Theatre Bench in assoc
for the Finborough Thea

The World Premiere

CARTHAGE

by **Chris Thompson**

FINBOROUGH | THEATRE

First performed at the Finborough Theatre as a staged reading as part of *Vibrant 2012 – A Festival of Finborough Playwrights*: Thursday, 15 November 2012.

First performed at the Finborough Theatre: Tuesday, 28 January 2014.

Chris Thompson is the Channel 4 Playwrights Scheme Playwright in Residence at the Finborough Theatre, sponsored by Channel 4 Television and supported by The Peggy Ramsay Foundation.

CARTHAGE

by **Chris Thompson**

Cast in order of speaking

Tommy Anderson	**Jack McMullen**
Anne Anderson	**Claire-Louise Cordwell**
Marcus Reeves	**Toby Wharton**
Sue Ruskin	**Lisa Palfrey**
Karin Francis	**Elaine Claxton**
Simon Gale/Lou Martel	**Oliver Jackson**
Alex Sutherland	**Chinna Wodu**

The action takes place in London, 1998 to 2013.
The performance lasts approximately eighty minutes.
There will be no interval.

Director	**Robert Hastie**
Designer	**James Perkins**
Lighting Designer	**Gary Bowman**
Casting Directors	**Alastair Coomer CDG** **Vicky Richardson**
Fight Director	**Philip d'Orléans**
Production Manager	**Bernd Fauler**
Stage Manager	**Sophie Goody**
Associate Designer	**Sophia Simensky**
Assistant Director	**Hannah Jones**
Assistant Lighting Designer	**Jack Weir**
Production Electrician/Programmer	**Dan Street**
Producer	**Jim Zalles**
Associate Producer	**Lauren McGee**

Our patrons are respectfully reminded that, in this intimate theatre, any noise such as rustling programmes, talking or the ringing of mobile phones may distract the actors and your fellow audience-members.

We regret there is no admittance or re-admittance to the auditorium whilst the performance is in progress.

Elaine Claxton | Karin Francis
Theatre includes *Beasts and Beauties* (Hampstead Theatre), *Nation, The Relapse, A Winter's Tale, Richard II, The Relapse* and *The Children's Hour* (National Theatre).
Television includes *Wire In The Blood, Doc Martin, A Dinner of Herbs* and *Waking The Dead.*

Claire-Louise Cordwell | Anne Anderson
Trained at RADA.
Theatre includes *Dangerous Lady* (Theatre Royal, Stratford East), *Beautiful Thing* (Royal Exchange Theatre, Manchester), *The Swan* (National Theatre), *There is a War* (National Theatre), *Ecstasy* (Hampstead Theatre and Duchess Theatre), *Oleanna* (Theatre Royal York), *Orphans* (Paines Plough), *The Frontline* (Shakespeare's Globe), *Othello* (Frantic Assembly), *Torn* (Arcola Theatre), *Dirty Butterfly* (The Young Vic), *Days of Significance* (Royal Shakespeare Company at the Tricycle Theatre), *Burn / Chatroom / Citizenship* (National Theatre), *Stoning Mary* (Royal Court Theatre) and *Compact Failure* (Clean Break).
Film includes *Snow in Paradise*, *Stuart: A Life Backwards* and *The Curry Club*.
Television includes *Line of Duty*, *The Honourable Woman*, *Holby City*, *Call the Midwife*, *Casualty*, *Doctors*, *The Bill*, *Law and Order UK*, *Day of the Triffids*, *EastEnders*, *Trial and Retribution*, *Jane Hall's Big Bad Bus Ride* and *Bad Girls.*

Oliver Jackson | Simon Gale / Lou Martel
Theatre includes *She Stoops To Conquer* (National Theatre), *The Glee Club* (Bush Theatre and Duchess Theatre), *Our House* (Cambridge Theatre), *Les Miserables* (Palace Theatre), *Erics* (Everyman Theatre, Liverpool), *A Funny Thing Happened On The Way To The Forum* (New Wolsey Theatre, Ipswich), *Alice In Wonderland* (West Yorkshire Playhouse) and two seasons at the Open Air Theatre, Regent's Park.
Film includes *Redirected*, *Entity*, *Les Miserables* and *Unlawful Killing*.
Television includes *Law and Order UK*, *Murderland*, *He Kills Coppers*, *Dalziel and Pascoe, The Bill*, *Doctors*, *2:4 Children* and *Peak Practice*.

Jack McMullen | Tommy Anderson
Theatre includes *The Loneliness of the Long Distance Runner* (Pilot Theatre at Theatre Royal York).
Film includes *Seamonsters* and *The Hatching.*
Television includes *Waterloo Road, Moving On, The Street* and *Casualty.*

Lisa Palfrey | Sue Ruskin
Theatres includes *Before It Rains* (Bristol Old Vic and Sherman Cymru, Cardiff), *Canvas* (Chichester Festival Theatre), *The Kitchen Sink* (Bush Theatre), *Red Bud* (Royal Court Theatre), *Ingredient X* (Royal Court Theatre), *Small Change* (Sherman Cymru, Cardiff), *Blink* (Tour and Off-Broadway for FAB Theatre Company), *Gathered Dust And Dead Skin* (Live Theatre, Newcastle), *Festen* (Lyric Theatre and Almeida Theatre), *Under The Blue Sky* (Royal Court Theatre), *The Iceman Cometh* (Almeida Theatre), *Cardiff East* (National Theatre), *Under Milk Wood* (National Theatre), *Yerma* (National Theatre Studio), *The Story of an African Farm* (National Theatre Studio), *Ghosts* (Sherman Cymru, Cardiff) and *House of America* (National Tour).
Film includes *Pride*, *Maybe Baby*, *Guest House Paradiso*, *House of America*, *The Deadness of Dad* and *The Englishman Who Went Up A Hill But Came Down A Mountain.*
Television includes *Family Tree*, *Blodau*, *The Inspector Lynley Mysteries*, *The Bill*, *Armadillo*, *Casualty*, *Green Eyed Monster*, *Magistrates*, *Mind Games* and *Split Second*.

Toby Wharton | Marcus Reeves
At the Finborough Theatre, Toby co-wrote and appeared in *Fog* (2012) and appeared in *His Greatness* (2012) and *Carthage* as part of *Vibrant 2012 – A Festival of Finborough Playwrights*.
Trained at RADA.
Theatre includes *Home* (National Theatre), *Days of Significance* (Royal Shakespeare Company), *Fog* (National Tour), *Shalom Baby* (Theatre Royal, Stratford East), *Ajax* (Riverside Studios), and *Transient* (Pleasance Edinburgh and Shunt Vaults).
Film includes *Absence*, *Echo Road*, *Postcode* and *Bashment.*
Television includes *Gates, Silent Witness* and *The Bill.*

Chinna Wodu | Alex Sutherland
Theatre includes *Julius Caesar* (Royal Shakespeare Company at the Noël Coward Theatre), *Dr Faustus, Troilus and Cressida* (Shakespeare's Globe), *Italian Dreams, Teach Me* (Soho Theatre) and *Macbeth* (Royal Exchange Theatre, Manchester).
Television includes *Da Vinci's Demons*.

Chris Thompson | Playwright
Chris is the Channel 4 Playwright in Residence at the Finborough Theatre, where he makes his professional debut with *Carthage.* The play has won Chris a Channel 4 Playwright's Scheme bursary (formerly the Pearson Playwright Award), judged by a panel including Sir Richard Eyre CBE, Michael Billington OBE and Indhu Rubasingham. The Finborough Theatre premiered an earlier version of *Carthage* as part of *Vibrant 2012 – A Festival of Finborough Playwrights,* the Finborough Theatre's annual festival of new writing. In 2013, Chris was invited to take part in the Royal Court Theatre's Studio Writers' Group and the Kudos/Bush Initiative. He is currently under commission to the Bush Theatre.

Robert Hastie | Director
Productions at the Finborough Theatre include *Events While Guarding the Bofors Gun* (2012), a staged reading of *Photos of You Sleeping* as part of the *Papatango New Writing Prize* (2012) and the original staged reading of *Carthage* as part of *Vibrant 2012 – A Festival of Finborough Playwrights*.
Other directing includes the UK premiere of *Sunburst* by Tennessee Williams as part of *The Hotel Plays* at Holborn Grange Hotel, and as co-director, *As You Like It* and *A Midsummer Night's Dream* for the Lamb Players. Associate Direction includes *Coriolanus* and the forthcoming *Privacy* at the Donmar Warehouse, *Sixty-Six Books* which opened the new Bush Theatre, where he directed world premieres including *In The Land of Uz* by Neil LaBute and *The Middle Man* by Anthony Weigh, and *Much Ado About Nothing* at the Wyndham's Theatre.
Robert is Trainee Associate Director at the Donmar Warehouse.

James Perkins | Designer
Productions at the Finborough Theatre include *Trying* (2009), *Foxfinder* (2011) and *Events While Guarding the Bofors Gun* (2012).
Other theatre includes *Floyd Collins* (Southwark Playhouse), *The Girl in The Yellow Dress* (Salisbury Playhouse), *The Fantasist's Waltz* (Theatre Royal York), *Matters of Life and Death* (National Tour), *Many Moons* (Theatre503), *Beowulf* (Charles Court Opera), *Stockwell* (Tricycle Theatre), *The Marriage of Figaro* (Wilton's Music Hall), *Saraband* (Jermyn Street Theatre), *Girls and Dolls*, *Colourings* (Old Red Lion Theatre), *Iolanthe*, *Through The Woods* (Pleasance London), *The Pirates of Penzance*, *HMS Pinafore* (Buxton Opera House), *The Barber*

(Greenwich Theatre), *The Wonder* (BAC), *The Only True History of Lizzie Finn* (Southwark Playhouse), *St John's Night* (Jermyn Street Theatre) and *Lost in Yonkers* (Watford Palace Theatre). James created Story Whores.

Gary Bowman | Lighting Designer
Productions at the Finborough Theatre include *Apart from George* (2009), *S-27* (2009), *Foxfinder* (2011) and *A Life* (2012).
Trained at Bristol Old Vic Theatre School.
Gary has been Deputy Chief Electrician at the Donmar Warehouse, worked as an electrician on productions including *Wicked*, *Rock of Ages*, *Chicago* and he is currently on the Royal Shakespeare Company's production of *Matilda* in the West End.
Theatre includes *Ciphers* (Bush Theatre and National Tour), *Mana* (The Place and National Tour), *Thark* (Park Theatre), *Even Stillness Breathes Softly Against A Brick Wall* (Soho Theatre), *Liar Liar, 1001 Nights* (Unicorn Theatre), *Feathers in the Snow, The Only True History of Lizzie Finn* (Southwark Playhouse), *The Disappearance of Sadie Jones* (Bikeshed Theatre and National Tour), *Angle at the Bush* (Bush Theatre), *Life for Beginners* (Theatre503), *Gotcha, Mary Rose, The Art of Concealment* (Riverside Studios), *Jest End* (Jermyn Street Theatre), *Leopoldville, Stuff* (Tristan Bates Theatre), *Present Laughter* (Maddermarket Theatre, Norwich), *Miss Julie* (Attic Theatre, Stratford Upon-Avon), *Angel, The Muse* (Pleasance London) and *Ordinary Lads* (Etcetera Theatre).

Sophia Simensky | Assistant Designer
Productions at the Finborough Theatre include Costume Designer for *Events Whilst Guarding the Bofors Gun* (2012) and *Lost Boy* (2014), and Set and Costume Designer for *An Incident at the Border* (2012) – and its subsequent transfer to Trafalgar Studios – and *Operation Crucible* (2013).
Trained at Wimbledon College of Art.
Theatre includes *Cape* (Unicorn Theatre), *The Altitude Brothers* (Redbridge Arts Centre), *The Tailor-Made Man* (Arts Theatre), *Burning Bird* (Unicorn Theatre), *Oranges on the Brain* (Pegasus Theatre, Oxford), and *You and Me* (Greenwich Theatre).
Film includes *Screaming Guns*.

Philip d'Orléans | Fight Director
Philip is a member of the Equity Register of Fight Directors, and of the teaching and examining staff of the British Academy of Stage and Screen Combat. He has worked throughout Europe and America, alongside his regular teaching commitments for RADA, Drama Studio London and other drama schools and universities.
Theatre includes *Henry IV, Parts I and II*, *God of Soho*, *The Mysteries*, *A Midsummer Night's Dream*, *Macbeth*, *A New World* and *Othello* (Shakespeare's Globe), *Julius Caesar* and *I'll Be The Devil* (Royal Shakespeare Company), *Simon Boccanegra*, *Faust* and *Ariodante* (English National Opera), *Veneziana*, *L'Isola Disabitata* and *Der Rosenkavalier* (Royal Opera House), *Swimming With Sharks* (Vaudeville Theatre), *Cool Hand Luke* (Aldwych Theatre), *Carrie's War* (Apollo Theatre), *Merlin*, *Robin Hood* (Dukes Theatre, Lancaster), *King Lear* (Theatre Royal, Bath), *The Widowing of Mrs. Holroyd*, *Far From The Madding Crowd*, *The Rivals*, *Desire Under The Elms*, *Bleak House* and *Humble Boy* (New Vic Theatre, Newcastle-under-Lyme), *Othello*, *A Midsummer Night's Dream*, *Cyrano de Bergerac*, *Masters Are You Mad?*, *Twelfth Night*, *Merlin* (Grosvenor Park Open Air Theatre, Chester), *L'Olympiade* (Garsington Opera), *A View From The Bridge*, *King David*, *The Grapes Of Wrath*, *Romeo and Juliet*, *Coriolanus*, *Julius Caesar*, *Lonesome West*, *IPH*, *Journey's End* and *Aladdin* (Mercury Theatre, Colchester), *Death and the Maiden*, *Arsenic and Old Lace*, *What the Butler Saw*, *People at Sea*, *The Herbal Bed*, *Robin Hood*, *Shadowlands*, *Sleeping Beauty*, *Two Cities*, *Playing For Time*, *To Kill A Mockingbird*, *Cinderella*, *Jamaica Inn*, *Aladdin* and *The Hired Man* (Salisbury Playhouse),
Film includes *The Knife That Killed Me* (Universal Pictures).

Bernd Fauler | Production Manager
Trained in Stage Management at Rose Bruford College.
Theatre includes *The Roundabout Auditorium, Jumpers For Goalposts, Good With People, Wasted, 65 Miles* (Paines Plough), *No Place To Go, Dances Of Death, Purple Heart, The Trojan Women, Sunset Baby*, *The Prophet* (Gate Theatre), *SPILL Festival 2013* (Pacitti Company), *Once Upon A Time In Wigan, Krapp's Last Tape, Spoonface Steinberg* (Hull Truck Theatre), *Open East* (Create London at the Barbican), *The Fidget Project* (London Arts in Health Forum and Wellcome Trust), *Access All Areas, Performance Matters 2011 and 2012* (Live Art Development Agency), *SACRED* 2009 and 2010 (Chelsea

Theatre), *London via Lagos* Season (Ovalhouse), *Duckie Goes To The Gateways, Gross Indecency, Duckie* (Latitude Festival), *Hurts Given and Received, Slowly* (The Wrestling School), and *Where's My Desi Soulmate?, It Ain't All Bollywood, Meri Christmas, The Deranged Marriage* (Rifco Arts).

Sophie Goody | Stage Manager
Productions at the Finborough Theatre include *Events While Guarding The Bofors Gun* (2012) and *Hard Feelings* (2013). Theatre includes *My Mother Is a Fish* (Suspense Festival), *Bloodshot* (Canterbury Festival), *Land Of Our Fathers* (Theatre503), *My Favourite Madman* (Edinburgh Festival), *Desolate Heaven* (Theatre503), *A Christmas Fair* (English Touring Theatre), *The Hotel Plays* (Defibrillator), *I Am A Camera* (Paulden Hall Productions) and *The Alchemist* (Dunnico Theatre).

Hannah Jones | Assistant Director
Hannah is currently Resident Assistant Director at the Finborough Theatre where she has been Assistant Director for *The White Carnation* (2013), *Fishskin Trousers* (2013), *The Precariat* (2013) and *The Pavilion* as part of *Vibrant 2013 – A Festival of Finborough Playwrights.*
Trained at The University of Winchester.
Theatre includes *For a Look or a Touch* (King's Head Theatre), *A Midsummer Night's Dream*, *Mannequins* and *Playhouse Creatures* (The Studio, Winchester).

FINBOROUGH | THEATRE

VIBRANT **NEW WRITING** | UNIQUE **REDISCOVERIES**

"Audacious and successful... West London's Finborough Theatre is one of the best in the entire world. Its programme of new writing and obscure rediscoveries remains 'jaw-droppingly good'". ***Time Out***

"A disproportionately valuable component of the London theatre ecology. Its programme combines new writing and revivals, in selections intelligent and audacious." ***Financial Times***

"The Finborough Theatre, under the artistic direction of Neil McPherson, has been earning a place on the must-visit list with its eclectic, smartly curated slate of new works and neglected masterpieces" ***Vogue***

Founded in 1980, the multi-award-winning Finborough Theatre presents plays and music theatre, concentrated exclusively on vibrant new writing and unique rediscoveries from the 19th and 20th centuries. Behind the scenes, we continue to discover and develop a new generation of theatre makers – through our Literary team, and our programmes for both interns and Resident Assistant Directors.

Despite remaining completely unsubsidised, the Finborough Theatre has an unparalleled track record of attracting the finest creative talent who go on to become leading voices in British theatre. Under Artistic Director Neil McPherson, it has discovered some of the UK's most exciting new playwrights including Laura Wade, James Graham, Mike Bartlett, Sarah Grochala, Jack Thorne, Simon Vinnicombe, Alexandra Wood, Al Smith, Nicholas de Jongh and Anders Lustgarten; and directors including Blanche McIntyre.

Artists working at the theatre in the 1980s included Clive Barker, Rory Bremner, Nica Burns, Kathy Burke, Ken Campbell, Jane Horrocks and Claire Dowie. In the 1990s, the Finborough Theatre first became known for new writing including Naomi Wallace's first play *The War Boys*; Rachel Weisz in David Farr's *Neville Southall's Washbag*; four plays by Anthony Neilson including *Penetrator* and *The Censor*, both of which transferred to the Royal Court Theatre; and new plays by Richard Bean, Lucinda Coxon, David Eldridge, Tony Marchant and Mark Ravenhill. New writing development included the premieres of modern classics such as Mark Ravenhill's *Shopping and F***ing*, Conor McPherson's *This Lime Tree Bower*, Naomi Wallace's *Slaughter City* and Martin McDonagh's *The Pillowman.*

Since 2000, new British plays have included Laura Wade's London debut *Young Emma*, commissioned for the Finborough Theatre; two one-woman shows by Miranda Hart; James Graham's *Albert's Boy* with Victor Spinetti; Sarah Grochala's *S27*; Peter Nichols' *Lingua Franca*, which transferred Off-Broadway; and West End transfers for Joy Wilkinson's *Fair*; Nicholas de Jongh's *Plague Over England*; and Jack Thorne's *Fanny and Faggot*. The late Miriam Karlin made her last stage appearance in *Many Roads to Paradise* in 2008.
UK premieres of foreign plays have included Brad Fraser's *Wolfboy*; Lanford Wilson's *Sympathetic Magic*; Larry Kramer's *The Destiny of Me*; Tennessee Williams' *Something Cloudy, Something Clear*; the English premiere of Robert McLellan's Scots language classic, *Jamie the Saxt*; and three West End transfers – Frank McGuinness' *Gates of Gold* with William Gaunt and John Bennett; Joe DiPietro's *F***ing Men*; and Craig Higginson's *Dream of the Dog* with Dame Janet Suzman.

Rediscoveries of neglected work – most commissioned by the Finborough Theatre – have included the first London revivals of Rolf Hochhuth's *Soldiers* and *The Representative*; both parts of Keith Dewhurst's *Lark Rise to Candleford*; *The Women's War*, an evening of original suffragette plays; *Etta Jenks* with Clarke Peters and Daniela Nardini; Noël Coward's first play, *The Rat Trap*; Charles

Wood's *Jingo* with Susannah Harker; Emlyn Williams' *Accolade*; Lennox Robinson's *Drama at Inish* with Celia Imrie and Paul O'Grady; John Van Druten's *London Wall* which transferred to St James' Theatre; and J. B. Priestley's *Cornelius* which transferred to a sell out Off Broadway run in New York City.

Music Theatre has included the new (premieres from Grant Olding, Charles Miller, Michael John LaChuisa, Adam Guettel, Andrew Lippa, Paul Scott Goodman, and Adam Gwon's *Ordinary Days* which transferred to the West End) and the old (the UK premiere of Rodgers and Hammerstein's *State Fair* which also transferred to the West End, and the acclaimed 'Celebrating British Music Theatre' series, reviving forgotten British musicals.

The Finborough Theatre won *The Stage* Fringe Theatre of the Year Award in 2011, *London Theatre Reviews'* Empty Space Peter Brook Award in 2010 and 2012, the Empty Space Peter Brook Award's Dan Crawford Pub Theatre Award in 2005 and 2008, the Empty Space Peter Brook Mark Marvin Award in 2004, and swept the board with eight awards at the 2012 OffWestEnd Awards including Best Artistic Director and Best Director for the second year running. *Accolade* was named Best Fringe Show of 2011 by *Time Out*. It is the only unsubsidised theatre ever to be awarded the Pearson Playwriting Award (now the Channel 4 Playwrights Scheme) nine times. Three bursary holders (Laura Wade, James Graham and Anders Lustgarten) have also won the Catherine Johnson Award for Pearson Best Play.

www.finboroughtheatre.co.uk

FINBOROUGH | THEATRE

VIBRANT **NEW WRITING** | UNIQUE **REDISCOVERIES**

118 Finborough Road, London SW10 9ED
admin@finboroughtheatre.co.uk
www.finboroughtheatre.co.uk

Artistic Director | **Neil McPherson**

Resident Designer | Deputy Chief Executive | **Alex Marker**

General Managers | **Alice Krijgsman** and **Winona Navin-Holder**

Assistant General Managers | **Gill Daniell** and **Katharina Reinthaller**

Pearson Playwright-in-Residence | **Shamser Sinha**

Channel 4 Playwright-in-Residence | **Chris Thompson**

Playwrights-in-Residence | **Bekah Brunstetter**, **James Graham**, **Dawn King**, **Anders Lustgarten** and **Shamser Sinha**

Playwrights on Attachment | **Steven Hevey** and **Louise Monaghan**
Literary Manager | **Francis Grin**

Senior Reader | **Reen Polonsky**

Literary Assistant | **Miran Hadzic**

Literary Associate Music Theatre | **Max Pappenheim**

Associate Designer | **Philip Lindley**

Resident Casting Directors | **Lucy Casson**, **Hayley Kaimakliotis**

Resident Assistant Directors | **Mark Dominy** and **Hannah Jones**

And our many interns and volunteers.

The Finborough Theatre has the support of the Channel 4 Playwrights' Scheme, sponsored by Channel 4 Television and supported by The Peggy Ramsay Foundation

The Finborough Theatre is a member of the Independent Theatre Council, Musical Theatre Network UK and The Earl's Court Society www.earlscourtsociety.org.uk

Mailing
Email admin@finboroughtheatre.co.uk or give your details to our Box Office staff to join our free email list. If you would like to be sent a free season leaflet every three months, just include your postal address and postcode

Follow Us Online

www.facebook.com/FinboroughTheatre
www.twitter.com/finborough

Feedback
We welcome your comments, complaints and suggestions. Write to Finborough Theatre, 118 Finborough Road, London SW10 9ED or email us at admin@finboroughtheatre.co.uk

Playscripts
Many of the Finborough Theatre's plays have been published and are on sale from our website.

Finborough Theatre T-Shirts are now on sale from the Box Office, available in Small and Medium £7.00.

Smoking is not permitted in the auditorium and the use of cameras and recording equipment is strictly prohibited.

In accordance with the requirements of the Royal Borough of Kensington and Chelsea:

1. The public may leave at the end of the performance by all doors and such doors must at that time be kept open.

2. All gangways, corridors, staircases and external passageways intended for exit shall be left entirely free from obstruction whether permanent or temporary.

3. Persons shall not be permitted to stand or sit in any of the gangways intercepting the seating or to sit in any of the other gangways.

The Finborough Theatre is licensed by the Royal Borough of Kensington and Chelsea to The Steam Industry, a registered charity and a company limited by guarantee. Registered in England and Wales no. 3448268. Registered Charity no. 1071304. Registered Office: 118 Finborough Road, London SW10 9ED.

The Steam Industry is under the overall Artistic Direction of Phil Willmott. www.philwillmott.co.uk

Friends

The Finborough Theatre is a registered charity. We receive no public funding, and rely solely on the support of our audiences. Please do consider supporting us by becoming a member of our Friends of the Finborough Theatre scheme. There are four categories of Friends, each offering a wide range of benefits.

Brandon Thomas Friends – David Alpers. The Beryls. Penelope H. Bridgers. David Day. Mike Frohlich. Bill Hornby. Barbara Marker. Barbara Naughton. Sally Posgate. Michael Rangos. Nick Salaman. Barry Serjent.

Richard Tauber Friends – James Brown. Tom Erhardt. Bill Hornby. Richard Jackson. Mike Lewendon. John Lawson. Harry MacAuslan. Mark and Susan Nichols. Sarah Thomas.

Lionel Monckton Friends – S. Harper. Philip G Hooker. M. Kramer. Maxine and Eric Reynolds.

William Terriss Friends – Stuart Ffoulkes. Leo and Janet Liebster. Peter Lobl. Paul Kennedy. Corinne Rooney. Jon and NoraLee Sedmak.

CARTHAGE

Chris Thompson

CARTHAGE

OBERON BOOKS
LONDON

WWW.OBERONBOOKS.COM

First published in 2014 by Oberon Books Ltd
521 Caledonian Road, London N7 9RH
Tel: +44 (0) 20 7607 3637 / Fax: +44 (0) 20 7607 3629
e-mail: info@oberonbooks.com
www.oberonbooks.com

A catalogue record for this book is available from the British Library.

PB ISBN: 978-1-78319-069-0
E ISBN: 978-1-78319-568-8

Printed and bound by Marston Book Services, Didcot.

For Marie

Characters

ANNE ANDERSON

TOMMY ANDERSON, Anne's son

MARCUS REEVES, a prison officer and Tommy's case worker

SUE RUSKIN, Tommy's social worker

SIMON GALE, Anne's case worker in prison

KARIN FRANCIS, governor of a young offender's institute

ALEX SUTHERLAND, a prison officer

LOU MARTEL, a prison officer

POLICE OFFICER(s)

PRISON OFFICER(s)

The action takes place in the time between ANNE being 15 and 30, though not chronologically. The final scene takes place in the present day.

A speech with no dialogue and '–' indicates a character deliberately remaining silent or struggling to find the words.

Speeches which end with '–' are interrupted by the subsequent character.

1.

A mother and her teenage son in a fixed embrace. There is no time or place.

TOMMY: Will you bring my trainers?

ANNE: Yeah.

TOMMY: I'll write though.

ANNE: It's alright, Tommy.

TOMMY: Me Nike ones, yeah?

ANNE: They'll get robbed.

TOMMY: No they won't. Come visit me, mum, yeah?

ANNE: *(Tightens her embrace.)* Come 'ere.

TOMMY: *(Laughing.)* I can't breathe, Mum!

ANNE: Don't lie.

TOMMY: Me Nike ones, mum, yeah?

ANNE: Yeah, your Nike ones, I know.

TOMMY: When will you come up?

ANNE: Soon.

TOMMY: You'll come up though?

ANNE: Yeah, I'll be up.

TOMMY: When though?

ANNE: Soon. Dunno.

TOMMY: With me trainers?

ANNE squeezes him tighter still.

TOMMY: Mum? Me trainers, mum.

ANNE: Go on, off you go.

2.

Prison. MARCUS is sat in a room with a TV on the table in front of him. He sits in silence for a time. Enter SUE.

MARCUS: Well?

SUE: I'm just back from there now.

MARCUS: How is she?

SUE: How would you be?

Sorry.

She's pretty bad.

I just came back to say that she knows.

MARCUS: Should I call her or something?

SUE: I didn't give her your name.

MARCUS: She might want to speak to me though. Do you think she'll want to speak to me?

SUE: Are you ok?

MARCUS: I don't know what the decent thing to do is.

SUE: Do you have someone at home? A partner or –

MARCUS: Girlfriend.

SUE: That's good. Does she know?

MARCUS: She's picking me up.

SUE: That's good.

Enter KARIN.

KARIN: Who's she?

MARCUS: The social worker.

KARIN: Does she know?

SUE: Of course I know.

KARIN: The mum.

SUE: I'm just back from there now.

KARIN: Did she mention legal action, or solicitors? Anything like that?

SUE: She was pretty bad.

KARIN: Sure, of course. But did she mention legal action?

SUE: No.

I did.

KARIN: I'm gonna need to speak to Marcus on his own. If you go through that door, they'll escort you.

SUE: Marcus, are you going to be ok?

KARIN: Just that door there. Thank you.

MARCUS: You just get to leave then.

SUE: Excuse me, Marcus, I'm not the –

Sorry.

KARIN: Just through that door – Sue, it is?

SUE: Is he ok? He looks terrible.

KARIN: He's fine. Leave it with me.

SUE: If I can do anything –

MARCUS: Can you just get her out of here please?

KARIN: He'll be fine.

Exit SUE.

MARCUS: What about the press?

KARIN: The statement goes out tomorrow.

MARCUS: And?

KARIN: We're still working on the language.

Marcus, I'm going to need you to have another look at your version of events.

MARCUS: I've already given an account.

KARIN: The police are going to be back here first thing for your statements. And the difficulty as I see it now is that all three of you have given accounts to me and none of them match.

MARCUS: How is that my fault? Karin, I haven't lied.

KARIN: Of course not. All the same I want to see if we can bring some unity to what messages are coming from this building.

MARCUS: Unity?

KARIN: Unity, yes. I'm wondering if I gave you a chance to watch the footage. Informally. Let you see things from an objective viewpoint, it might help you put your thoughts in a more unified order.

MARCUS: It's an impossible job. No wonder someone gets hurt.

KARIN: Marcus. Why didn't you stop? Is it –

MARCUS: No.

KARIN: It was a serious crime. That must be hard to work with.

MARCUS: Yeah it's hard to work with. So what?

KARIN: There were calls in the press for –

MARCUS: I know. So what?

KARIN: I'm planning on saying that restraining children allows a deep and profound trust to develop between child and professional. It's actually quite a caring action.

MARCUS: And you believe that do you?

KARIN: Do I believe what?

MARCUS: All what you just said.

KARIN: I don't think that's the most important question at the moment.

MARCUS: You want me to change my statement to say that a deep and profound trust developed between me and Tommy when I restrained him?

KARIN: I'm saying that's what these restraint techniques enable.

MARCUS: It's bullshit.

KARIN: We have a restraint policy in this unit.

MARCUS: So why are you pinning it on me?

KARIN: We have a restraint policy in this unit.

MARCUS: And I did it right.

KARIN: Why don't I just pop the tape in?

MARCUS: I'm really not ready to see it, Karin.

KARIN: Give me a commentary on what you see.

KARIN puts in a tape and gets a notepad and pen ready.

MARCUS: That's when he attacked me.

KARIN: What was his mood like today? Any changes in behaviour?

MARCUS: He'd been volatile but no more than usual.

KARIN: How many times has he been restrained since he got here?

MARCUS: He's been volatile, I just told you.

KARIN: Good. That's helpful to know.

And what about now? What's happening now?

MARCUS: The other two have entered and we've started to restrain him.

KARIN: And he resisted?

MARCUS: They always resist.

KARIN: And whose decision was it to continue with the restraint?

MARCUS: You're not meant to stop midway through.

KARIN: So this is when he vomits, and I also understand it was at this point he defecated. Whose decision was it to continue with the restraint after that?

MARCUS: I can't remember.

KARIN: Are you telling me you can't remember back that far?

MARCUS: I can't remember what we said. There was a lot of confusion.

KARIN: The images show you looking at Tommy's face then reporting back to your colleagues. Do you recall offering an assessment, or any form of instruction about whether to continue with the restraint or to stop it all together?

MARCUS: I don't recall that.

KARIN: I can see you doing it.

MARCUS: You can see an assessment?

KARIN: I can see you talking.

MARCUS: We *are* talking.

KARIN: But are you offering an assessment on whether to stop or continue?

MARCUS: Jesus, fuck. I don't know, okay? What are you getting at?

KARIN: No one's saying it's anyone's fault at this stage, Marcus.

MARCUS: I'm not answering any more questions till I've spoken to a solicitor.

KARIN: People will want to know why you restrained him. You need to be prepared to answer that question.

MARCUS: We have a restraint policy in this unit.

He was born in a prison. Did you know that?

KARIN: Marcus, why didn't you stop the restraint?

MARCUS: I did it right.

KARIN: You're going to have to be absolutely certain that the restraint was legitimate. There need to be grounds, justifiable grounds, and this footage –

MARCUS: No, that footage shows me following the training to the letter.

KARIN: Early warning signs of asphyxiation ignored. We can't get away from the fact these images show what they show.

MARCUS: And I say what I say.

KARIN: What went on in there?

MARCUS: You've seen the tapes. You tell me.

KARIN: What went on in there?

MARCUS: I did what you taught me.

KARIN: Were the grounds for the restraint legitimate? You can't just go around attacking children.

MARCUS: I didn't attack him, that's a massive fucking leap, Karin – what are you saying?

KARIN: Did you give an instruction to continue?

MARCUS: I did it right.

KARIN: Did you deliberately ignore early warning signs of asphyxiation?

MARCUS: I did it right and he attacked me don't forget.

KARIN: Were you influenced by the crime Tommy was in here for?

MARCUS: –

KARIN: A boy is dead, Marcus.

MARCUS: Yes. A boy is dead, Karin.

KARIN: Marcus.

MARCUS: I know. Please don't say it anymore – I know. I know a boy is dead. And I know I did it right.

KARIN: *(Softly.)* I think if I was in your position, and I knew what he'd done. I don't think I can say for certain – given the chance – that I wouldn't want to –

3.

ANNE, SUE and SIMON in prison. ANNE, aged 15, is pregnant – at full term.

SUE: No.

SIMON: How many times do we have to go through this?

SUE: We've had this conversation.

SIMON: Sue agrees with me.

ANNE: Can I keep it or not?

SUE: What are we talking about here?

SIMON: Sue and I agree, don't we, Sue?

SUE: That depends.

ANNE: I wanna keep it. It's mine.

SIMON: You can't keep it, Anne.

SUE: Right, everyone stop. I'm talking about the baby. Simon, what are you talking about?

SIMON: The telly.

SUE: Anne, what are you talking about?

ANNE: The telly.

SUE: No, no, no. Anne, we agreed to discuss the baby first, then the TV. I put them in that order because it seemed sensible to discuss these things in order of priority, but I see I might have misjudged that.

ANNE: It's my telly. I want it back.

SUE: Baby first, then TV. Everyone got that?

ANNE: A month is too long.

SIMON: That's the sanction, Anne. We're not budging. You get it back in a month if your behaviour improves.

SUE: Stop. Everyone stop. Don't say anything, unless it's about what happens to this baby.

ANNE: There ain't gonna be no baby if I don't get my telly back.

SIMON: How do you plan on doing that?

SUE: Simon, can I speak to you alone for a minute please?

SIMON: Sure.

SIMON and SUE move away.

SUE: Is there any way she can have the TV back today?

SIMON: Why?

SUE: I'm just thinking of the bigger picture, Simon. We need to discuss the baby, and we won't move forward.

SIMON: It's been confiscated for a month. It's sorted.

SUE: If we can get her to co-operate, can we reward her with the TV?

SIMON: This fucking pregnancy. Do you realise what she's got away with because she's been pregnant? She knows we can't get physical with her so she's been pushing her luck.

SUE: The telly seems important to her.

SIMON: That's why we're taking it.

SUE: I'm about to give her some tough news, ok? The TV might –

ANNE: This is the news and these are the headlines, yeah. Sue and Simon are well gay. They are a pair of wankers, and they both take it up the bum, yeah, and Simon's all like, 'ah yeah, that feels well good, Sue, do me up the bum with a strap on some more, I'm like well your sex pig, aren't I?' And Sue, yeah, she's like all 'fuck yeah, smash my back door in, Simon'. And they all go round to Simon's house for a big gay paedo gang bang. They do do that though. And now the weather. It's gonna be well nice weather today.

SIMON: I thought a maternity wing was an option.

SUE: Even with that level of supervision, we think the baby will still be at too much risk at this stage. And even if she does manage for a while inside, once she gets out –

SIMON: She might manage.

SUE: It's too risky for now, Simon.

SIMON: It seems pretty severe, not to even give her a chance.

SUE: I don't mean to be rude, Simon, but comments like that are very easy to say on your side of things.

SIMON: Are you protecting the baby or are you protecting you?

SUE: Thanks, Simon, thanks for that. If there's an issue here –

SIMON: I'm just saying we have to take risks sometimes, and sometimes newer, less experienced social workers, no offence of course –

SUE: If you wanna take over this case, I will sign the paperwork and bring the files over to you and you can be responsible for the safety of the baby. Then let's see what risks you take.

Anne should look after her baby, there's no doubt as far as I'm concerned that that is the best thing for everyone. But for now I need to get the baby safe.

SIMON: Sorry, Sue. No TV.

ANNE: Do you like orgies?

SUE: Anne, you can't have the television today. Simon has made himself clear.

ANNE: I am getting the telly or not?

SIMON: No.

SUE: No.

ANNE: Can I go back to my cell now please?

SIMON: Sue needs to talk to you first.

ANNE: I know you are old, yeah and you don't understand what it is like being a teenager but teenagers like to watch telly you know and I want a telly in my cell, yeah, cos this prison is full of dirty bitches who keep movin' to me and I ain't no dyke so I need to stay in my cell where them lot can't touch me and Simon, yeah, you fuck your mum up her bum with your small dick, so give me my telly back, or I swear on my life I will tell the papers you lot made me go lesbo cos I ain't got nothing better to do in the pen.

SUE: Don't say Simon's got a small dick please, Anne. It's not polite. Men don't like it when women say men have small dicks, do they Simon?

SIMON: I don't know.

SUE: In fact, Simon, to help Anne fully understand the impact of her actions, maybe it would be useful for her to hear how it made you feel when she told you you had a small penis.

SIMON: Sue and I have spoken and we have agreed that you can keep the TV.

ANNE: I don't want your fucking telly.

SIMON: Fine, we'll take it back.

ANNE: I don't care, do I?

SUE: Okay well that seems sorted.

SIMON: Good. I'll keep it for two months.

SUE: Anne, we need to discuss the baby now.

ANNE: No we don't.

SUE: Yes we do, Anne. There's kind of a time limit going on here.

ANNE: I've met you two fucking times. Why would I speak to you?

SUE: Then you can just listen. As you know we've been doing an assessment –

ANNE: You ain't taking my telly for two months, you must be fucking joking. I'll call my solicitor.

SUE: So we did this assessment and –

ANNE: Dickheads.

SUE: And so the purpose of the assessment was to ascertain how well you could care for the baby. It's called a – oh, it's gone from me, anyway this assessment's got a name, and I know that we don't know each other all that well yet, so it must feel strange having someone come in and make all these recommendations but –

ANNE: Can I go back to my cell please?

SUE: No you can't. Sit down and shut your mouth young lady.

ANNE: You ain't allowed to speak to me like that, it ain't allowed.

SUE: Sorry. That just slipped out.

SIMON: Do you need some help, Sue?

SUE: Anne, aren't you interested in what is going to happen to you?

ANNE: No.

SIMON: I think you should be.

ANNE: Oh do you, Simon? Do you? Do you think I should give a shit what that bitch says about me. She don't know me. Do I look like I give a fuck?

SUE: I give up. I give up. Anne, I'm going now and I will write to you instead. I thought it was the decent thing to come and tell you to your face. We're going to have to work together, Anne. You need to engage with me.

ANNE: Tell me what to my face?

SUE: The outcome of my assessment.

ANNE: Well fucking say it then.

SUE: Not when you're like this.

ANNE: You lot can't say nothing to me.

ANNE gets up and grabs the telly.

SIMON: Get your hands off that young lady.

ANNE: It's mine.

SIMON: It's confiscated.

ANNE: No it fucking ain't.

SIMON: Anne.

SIMON and ANNE both have a hold of the telly. A stalemate.

SUE: Is there something good on tonight?

ANNE suddenly looks panicked. She begins to groan.

SIMON: Would someone give this girl an Oscar?

SUE: Anne? Is everything okay?

SIMON: Just ignore it.

ANNE: I think I've pissed myself.

SIMON: Shit. You could have warned us.

SUE: Where's the nurse?

SIMON: I'll get her. Hold on, Anne, darling. I'm gonna get someone who knows what to do.

ANNE: Hurry up.

SIMON runs out with his radio in hand. ANNE's groans become louder and more frequent as the following dialogue continues. SUE holds ANNE's hand.

SUE: It's okay, Anne. We'll get the nurse.

ANNE: Are you gonna let me keep it?

SUE: Don't think about that for now, Anne. Just concentrate on your contractions.

ANNE: What does that mean?

SUE: To be honest, I don't know. It's what they say on the telly – I'm not really trained for this side of things.

ANNE: I wanna keep it, Sue. Please, I won't let my dad near him.

SUE: Anne, listen to me. You know the score. Deep breaths and concentrate on your – you know.

ANNE: I just wanna keep my baby. Sue, please let me.

SUE: Anne.

ANNE: Can I keep him?

ANNE's groans and screams are at their loudest and most frequent.

Can I keep him?

SUE: Don't do this, Anne.

ANNE: Don't take him off me.

SIMON: The nurse is coming.

ANNE suddenly stops screaming, she's composed.

SIMON: Am I too late? Where's the bloody baby?

SUE: She's not in labour, Simon.

SIMON: I thought –

SUE: Yep, me too.

ANNE: Listen to me, yeah you donuts. You fucking talk like you own me, but you can fucking suck my pussy cos I ain't giving you my baby and you ain't takin' my telly.

4.

ANNE aged 15, is on a hospital-type bed in the healthcare wing. SUE stands at the end of the bed holding a baby.

SUE: Are you sure?

ANNE: –

SUE: I can –

ANNE: No.

SUE: You might find it useful.

I'm sorry, I know how that must sound.

He's beautiful. He's got your –

ANNE: No he don't.

SUE: Why don't you have a look, Anne? Hold him for a minute.

ANNE: No thank you.

SUE: They say holding your child in the moments after birth is –

ANNE: You hold a lot of other people's babies when they're born, do you?

SUE: It's good for attachment.

ANNE: You hold him then.

SUE: I am. But I'm saying you might want to. And we can take a picture for his memory book.

ANNE: I said no.

SUE: We're not saying permanent. I intend on seeing you raise this child, Anne, but you need to get things straight.

ANNE: I wanna live with my dad.

SUE: Then this isn't going to work.

ANNE: I'm not living there now.

SUE: No, you're living in a prison, Anne. You get yourself sorted when you're out and show to us you can care for him, then you can have him –

ANNE: I'm moving back in with dad.

SUE: Then there's no way you'll see this baby again.

ANNE: I'm good there.

SUE: You don't see anything wrong with the way you've been brought up, but I do, and you can't take a baby into that environment.

ANNE: Dad looks after me.

SUE: No, Anne, he doesn't.

ANNE: I like it there, Sue. Dad's been writing to me.

SUE: How? He's supposed to –

ANNE: You lot think you're clever, but you can't keep families apart.

SUE: I need to see those letters, Anne and actually, what I'm trying to do is keep your family together.

ANNE: Fuck off. All you need to know is that when we're both out, we'll be gone.

SUE: And this one? He's your family now too.

ANNE: I don't know, do I?

SUE: If you want to be a part of his life, we can look at that – make sure you see him lots so you build up a bond – permanent things. But if you wanna run off with dad, then you're saying goodbye to the baby, Anne.

ANNE: I'll find him.

SUE: No, Anne, I will find you. Go gallivanting around the country with daddy as much as you please but as long as you are a child, you are our responsibility and I will hunt you down young lady and drag you back kicking and screaming.

ANNE: I love it when you get cross, Sue.

SUE: I'm not cross, Anne, I'm fucking upset. I'm stood here with your baby who you won't even touch let alone give a name to and I've got to listen to your crap about you playing happy families with your excuse for a dad. This is not a bloody game, Anne. It's not about winning or getting your own way. It's about this baby.

ANNE: You name him.

SUE: Don't be ridiculous. Just hold him so I can take a picture for his memory book, would you?

ANNE: Tell me his name and I'll hold him.

SUE: This is not the time for deals.

ANNE: What's his name? I can't hold my child if I don't know his name.

SUE: Fine I'll name him if you like.

Tesco Value Chicken Cottage Poundland Anderson. Here you are, that's his name, say cheese it's photo time.

ANNE: I ain't calling him that.

SUE: We can shorten it I guess.

ANNE: Don't disrespect my baby, Sue.

SUE: Sorry, Anne, that's what happens when you leave these things to social workers. Say cheese, please, I'm parked in a disabled bay.

ANNE: I'm naming him.

SUE: Go on then.

ANNE: Tommy.

Tommy Anderson.

SUE takes a picture and gives ANNE and TOMMY a few moments.

SUE: Anne, you're going to find this strange, but I want you to know that we love you.

ANNE: No you don't. You get paid to do this.

SUE: Yes. I get paid to love you.

ANNE: Don't be gay.

SUE: Say bye to Tommy, Anne. If you change your mind about meeting the foster carers.

ANNE: He's got my eyes.

SUE: I know. He's a beautiful boy, Anne. Let's hope he hasn't got your herpes.

ANNE: Leave him here.

SUE: Tommy can't wait around indefinitely for you to get your shit together. You do get that at least, don't you?

ANNE: You shouldn't swear in front of children.

SUE: I would like to see him living with you, Anne.

ANNE: Leave him here with me.

SUE: And then what? This situation – it is what it is, I can't change that.

ANNE: When can I see him again?

SUE: With my hand on my heart, Anne, I don't know.

SUE leaves, taking TOMMY with her.

5.

An anteroom in a court building. MARCUS enters, bleeding. SUE follows him in quickly. Press cameras flash.

SUE: It's okay they've got her.

MARCUS: Fuck.

SUE: Let me see.

MARCUS: Did no one see her coming? She fucking went for me.

SUE: You're not okay, Marcus. I'll drive you to A&E.

MARCUS: No thanks.

SUE: Marcus, please, let me have a quick look.

MARCUS: I said I'm fine. Jesus.

SUE: You're not fine.

MARCUS: I don't need help from you.

SUE: Oh. I see. What's your girlfriend's name? I'll go and get her.

MARCUS: I don't need anything from you.

SUE: Given your position, you might –

MARCUS: My position? Hold on a minute, Sue.

SUE: You think this is *our* position?

MARCUS: Yes I do, actually, Sue, yes I do think this is our position.

SUE: I thought that might be the case.

MARCUS: You disappeared off the face of the earth soon enough.

SUE: Meaning?

MARCUS: Don't touch me, I don't need your help. Meaning I'm surprised you even showed up.

SUE: I counted how many times you said my name when you were on the stand.

Thirty-two.

That's very clever.

MARCUS: Yeah well it must be very comfortable in the gallery. You must get a good view of it all from up there.

SUE: And to try and put the blame on Tommy. That was quite a re-frame. It was pretty disgusting actually.

MARCUS: There were grounds, Sue.

SUE: You're allowed to fight back you know. If you're being attacked, you can defend yourself.

MARCUS: I don't want there to be any doubt when they watch the tapes back.

SUE: I wasn't talking about you. I meant Tommy. CCTV has served you rather well today all things considered.

MARCUS: You can just come out and say what you're thinking, Sue.

SUE: Are you going to press charges against Anne?

MARCUS: You think I shouldn't?

SUE: I think she's been through enough, yes. And today's verdict is hardly –

MARCUS: What about what I've been through, Sue? It's all right for you but it wasn't my fault he was inside, so yeah, you're damn right I said your name thirty-two times. And Anne's. The pair of you should have been in that dock.

I said, please don't touch me, I do not want your help.

SUE: Well in any case, it looks like you got away with it. That's a piece of good news, isn't it?

MARCUS: Got away with it. Is that what you think?

SUE: I think you said my name thirty-two times and then tried to blame all this on a child, so you can go fuck yourself, Marcus.

6.

The living room of a local authority flat. TOMMY is sat on the sofa watching The Jeremy Kyle Show. *He is wearing a plastic set of rosary beads. On a table in front of him are lines of cocaine. He is smoking a spliff and leans over and does a line. Now and again he laughs at the TV.*

TOMMY: *(To the television.)* Lie detector, lie detector! You ain't that bitch's father, I swear down you ain't.

Watches some more.

She don't even look like you. If my daughter was that ugly, I wouldn't take no lie detector test, you get me?

Does another line. Enter ANNE.

ANNE: Tommy! There's hardly none left. It's gotta last the weekend.

TOMMY: Yeah, but mum, it's been time since I done Charlie.

ANNE: That's my fault, is it? Here, clear off.

ANNE prepares a line and snorts it.

Welcome home, son. You being a good boy up there?

TOMMY: No.

ANNE: And why are we watching this crap?

TOMMY: What would you do, yeah, if you switched on *Jeremy Kyle* yeah mum, and there was me with this like, skanky Jez, and she was all like, you're my baby's babyfather yeah.

ANNE: What are you banging on about?

TOMMY: I'm just saying yeah, like for jokes, innit. What would you do if I was on The Jeremy Kyle show? It would be jokes, you get me? The lie detector's sick, Bruv. Man shits himself, yeah, cos he knows he's put his piece in some sket.

ANNE: Do your foster carers understand you? Christ, they should send you with a translator. Turn it over, would you? *Cash in the Attic*'s on.

TOMMY: That's moist, man, you're taking the piss.

ANNE: No Tommy, I am not taking the piss, I ain't having you watching low lifes on the telly. We don't watch that crap here. We watch better programmes.

TOMMY: Like Cash in the fucking Attic is a better programme. Fuck off!

A play fight over the remote control ensues. They are laughing, and at total ease in each other's company. They are also shit faced. Eventually there is a knock on the door. They both instinctively dive in front of the sofa to hide.

ANNE: Right on cue.

TOMMY: Fuck's sake.

ANNE: Is it definitely her?

TOMMY: It's her.

ANNE: She couldn't just leave it.

TOMMY: How did she find out?

ANNE: CCTV. I'll put money on it.

TOMMY: What are you talking about, mum?

ANNE: Hold on a minute. How did she find out what, Tommy?

TOMMY: Nothing. What couldn't she just leave, mum?

ANNE: Nothing. I lost my rag a bit. Nothing serious. Don't worry about it.

TOMMY: What have you done now, mum?

ANNE: Why do social workers always have to come when *Cash in the Attic*'s on? They do it deliberate, I swear.

TOMMY: Cos making me watch *Cash in the Attic* is child abuse. You always got to keep on bringing the social workers in our business.

ANNE: I pissed on her carpet.

TOMMY: When?

ANNE: I don't know, my darling. A week ago? She said I couldn't see you, so I went round and pissed on the office carpet.

TOMMY: I love you mum. But I hate Cash in the fucking Attic.

SUE is now peering through the window. TOMMY gets the remote, changes the channel back to Jeremy Kyle, *then flings the remote across the room so ANNE is unable to get it without being spotted. He pisses himself laughing.*

ANNE: Oh you are in so much trouble now. I am seriously gonna get you.

TOMMY: I ain't listening. This is abuse.

ANNE: How long is this gonna take? She's a letterbox talker this one.

TOMMY: Innit.

SUE opens the letterbox and begins to speak through. At some points during her speech, TOMMY and ANNE's hands appear and get things off the table – like the coke, or the ashtray. They settle in for the duration, unperturbed.

SUE: *(Through the letter box.)* Ah, *Jeremy Kyle.* He's my hero. Have they done the lie detector yet? I love that bit – when the guy's shitting himself cos he's been shagging some other bird on the side. You can't hide from the lie detector test.

So, here we all are. I think this must rank in my top five professional high points. Maybe even the top three. My number one involves you actually, Tommy. Do you remember when I came round that time and you picked me up, put me in the wheelie bin, then rolled me out to the end of the street? Oh, how we laughed that day. They don't tell you about that in the training, that's for sure.

Pause. Then sings badly.

I believe the children are our future
Teach them well and let them lead the way
Show them all the beauty they possess inside
Give them a sense of pride to make it easier
Let the children's...

ANNE gives up and goes to the door.

ANNE: Just one episode of *Cash in the Attic*, that's all I ask for.

SUE: Anne, how nice to see you. I think the telly must have been on a bit loud and you didn't hear me knocking.

ANNE: We was ignoring you until you went away.

SUE: You know me better than that, Anne. Tommy! You're alive. I've been up all night thinking about you.

ANNE: Tea?

SUE: Love one.

SUE goes to sit down and notices all the drugs on the table.

Actually, do you mind if I use your bathroom first?

TOMMY: It's through there.

SUE goes out. TOMMY and ANNE desperately clear all the drugs off the table and hide them. SUE comes back in.

ANNE: Tommy love, make us a cuppa, would you?

TOMMY: Why have I got to do it?

SUE: Because your mother says so.

TOMMY: Don't talk about me while I ain't there.

ANNE: Hurry up.

TOMMY goes out. SUE gets an envelope out of her bag. She opens it and empties its contents on the table. It is burnt ashes from the remains of a piece of paper that has been set fire to. SUE stares intently at ANNE.

ANNE: You had a fire, Sue?

SUE: Seriously? Is it seriously going to be like this?

ANNE: What was that? It looks –

SUE: It's the cleaning bill.

ANNE: What cleaning bill, Sue?

SUE: The one we sent you after you – Do we have to do this?

ANNE: It's hard to make out what is says cos in all fairness it looks like it's been set fire to or something. Are you sure it is the one you sent me, Sue?

SUE: I'm sure it is the one we sent you, Anne, yes.

ANNE: It doesn't look like the one you sent me.

SUE: Not now it doesn't, no, Anne. I agree with you.

ANNE: So?

SUE: Anne, I watched the CCTV footage – it was spectacular, don't get me wrong. But this is causing me no end of grief – you've made the receptionists go on strike. They think they're in a war zone.

ANNE: No it don't look nothing like the one you sent me.

SUE: Fortunately for you, Anne, I am a relentless bureaucrat, so I like to take copies. I find photocopying therapeutic. Perhaps instead of setting fire to this one in my reception area, you could pay it?

ANNE: What with?

SUE: Money, Anne. Most people tend to pay bills with money.

ANNE: You gonna press charges?

SUE: If we do you'll know about it.

ANNE: How've you been, Sue?

SUE: Yeah, I'm not bad, thanks Anne. Could do without chasing this one round the borough.

ANNE: So what, you expect me to turn my own son away every time he turns up?

SUE: No Anne, that's not –

ANNE: If you lot gave him his flat instead of them foster carers. He don't need foster carers, Sue, he needs his mum.

SUE: Oh my God, we go round in circles, Anne. Yes he needs his mum, you are absolutely right.

ANNE: He should be with white foster carers. If he comes back, he's got to stop talking black.

SUE: Do we seriously need to have this conversation again?

ANNE: Black foster carers should look after the black children and white –

SUE: White mothers should look after their own fucking white children, Anne. That's why I'm here. I wanted to catch you guys together, sound you out about whether Tommy moves back in with you. I thought it might be about time we had another go.

ANNE: Finally.

SUE: Tommy's saying he's ready to try again. He seems to have got over the taxi incident.

ANNE: I ain't making my boy get the bus.

SUE: This time can we agree that if you want to dump Tommy at my office again, you give me a call and I'll come and get him? We don't have the budget for taxis. And did it really have to be Addison Lee?

ANNE: They're a better class of taxi, Sue.

SUE: I know you love Tommy. I see the bond, but for all that love you've abandoned him three times, you have hit him, spat at him, and I have heard the messages you leave on his answer phone when you are under the influence. Those messages – they're hateful, and truthfully, Anne, I don't know how any mother can say those kinds of things about her son. People think I'm mad for letting him return to live with you.

ANNE: So why you still letting him live here if I'm so bad?

SUE: The reason I'm saying he can live with you is because, whether I like it or not, this is where he wants to be. I don't think it will last, I've got no problem telling you that.

ANNE: It will last, Sue.

SUE: What they're really worried about is the drugs. They think that you supply him. And I've been upfront with them, I've told them: you do supply Tommy with drugs, and it's not so much the drugs that bother me, it's what you say to him when you're off your face.

ANNE: He don't mind.

SUE: You're off your face now. You do know that I realise that don't you? So I mind for him. If you want him here, do all the drugs you like, I couldn't care less, but you shut your mouth when you are shitfaced from now on. Are you getting this? Stop leaving him those disgusting messages when you're battered.

ANNE: He knows I don't mean it.

SUE: Mean it or don't mean it, I couldn't give a shit, but don't speak like that to your child.

Enter TOMMY with tea.

TOMMY: Man's a tea expert. Got expertise in tea, you get me?

SUE: That looks lovely, thank you, Tommy.

ANNE: See, Sue? He loves his mum.

SUE: So, Tommy. Here you are.

TOMMY: I've gone AWOL, Sue.

SUE: You've not gone AWOL when you text me to say where you are. Not technically anyway.

ANNE: What you fucking texting her for?

TOMMY: Sue's a worrier, innit mum. Didn't want her to lose sleep.

SUE: I stopped losing sleep over you years ago, Tommy.

VOICES AT THE DOOR: Police! Open the door!

ANNE gets up to answer. TOMMY sprints into the kitchen.

ANNE: You couldn't wait could you? All I did was piss on a carpet.

SUE: What's going on, Anne?

ANNE opens the door, there are several POLICE OFFICERS. OFFICERS push past ANNE.

OFFICER: We are looking for Tommy Anderson, is he here?

ANNE: Tommy!

ANNE runs out into the kitchen.

SUE: I'm the family's social worker.

OFFICER: He's here then.

SUE: Yes. Why?

ANNE re-enters.

ANNE: He's gone.

SUE: What?

ANNE: He's not there, he's gone.

ONE OFFICER runs into the kitchen and then begins to search the rest of the flat, some run out the front door to search outside.

ANNE: What's he done now?

OFFICER: You the social worker?

SUE: *(Shows her ID badge.)* Are you going to answer Mrs Anderson's question?

OFFICER: Do you want to step outside a sec?

ANNE: No she fucking don't. What's going on?

SUE: I'll be two secs.

SUE and OFFICER walk out front door, the search continues around ANNE.

ANNE: I'm his fucking mother. I'm his fucking mother.

SUE re-enters. She looks shocked.

ANNE: I'm his fucking mother, Sue.

SUE: I know, Anne. Sit down.

ANNE: I'm his fucking mother. And you got to step outside to discuss my son?

SUE: Anne, will you just sit down, please.

ANNE: What the fuck is going on?

SUE: Anne, sit. Please.

ANNE and SUE sit.

It's bad.

7.

TOMMY is led in to a prison reception. He is brought to the desk where he is instructed to fill in several forms. He is then led to another desk. MARCUS is amongst the guards. KARIN is also present.

TOMMY's bag is emptied on to the desk and his belongings are searched.

Some things are taken off him and he has to sign for them.

TOMMY is then strip-searched by MARCUS.

When instructed, TOMMY first of all removes his top half clothes, puts his hands in the air and then turns around three hundred and sixty degrees back to face MARCUS.

He is then given a prison issue top to wear. Then follows his bottom half. He strips naked, hands his boxer shorts to MARCUS for inspection, turns around and when MARCUS is satisfied he gives TOMMY tracksuit bottoms and his boxers.

When dressed, he is given a plastic radio, toothbrush and paste and other similar items in a clear bag and is then told to wait.

MARCUS: This the one is it?

KARIN: Yeah. It's him.

MARCUS: Guilty then.

KARIN: And can't be named for legal reasons so watch what you're saying.

MARCUS: We get all the celebrities here, don't we? Follow me, Tommy. I've heard all about you.

MARCUS leads TOMMY to his cell, and follows him inside. As the door closes –

MARCUS: Welcome to Butlin's.

8.

In the visiting room of a prison.

ANNE (aged 30) sits alone at a table. She is wearing a prison issue nylon vest. PRISON OFFICERS circle the room. Eventually a PRISON OFFICER approaches ANNE.

PRISON OFFICER: If you want to go back let me know.

ANNE: It's not time yet.

PRISON OFFICER: Yes, I know. If you've had enough –

ANNE: No thanks.

PRISON OFFICER: I'm just saying, if you don't want to be down here, I can get you taken back. If he's not coming –

ANNE: No. Thank you.

Enter MARCUS. He gives his name at the desk and looks around the room. The PRISON OFFICER points out ANNE. He hesitates and then walks over slowly.

MARCUS: Mrs Anderson.

ANNE: Sit.

MARCUS: Sorry I'm late. I forgot how many doors you have to get through in these places. And I don't know why, but I expected the bus to bring us right to the gate. I just assumed as it said prison on it that that's where I'd end up. But there's a walk, and then it took forever to get through security. But here I am. Sorry I'm late.

ANNE: It don't take six months to get through security.

MARCUS: No.

ANNE: You still got the place near here?

MARCUS: –

ANNE: Spit it out man, I'm a busy woman. It's alright, it ain't like I can just pop in on my way back from the shops.

MARCUS: I've still got the place.

ANNE: At least you didn't have to come far. That's nice.

MARCUS: No, it's not far. I just thought the bus stopped closer to the gates, that's all.

ANNE: That makes us neighbours. That's nice for us, ain't it? A neighbourly visit.

MARCUS: That's not what this is.

ANNE: One thing I can say for this place, mind you, it don't half give you time to think. We done a poem about our favourite season, we did; and I wasn't sure at first: I never given it much thought before – these seasons, you know, they just come and go and you don't think nothing of it. But being here has let me really think about it. Get to the bottom of important shit like that.

MARCUS: Can't they teach you anything more useful?

ANNE: Your face healed alright then.

MARCUS: Apart from the scar. Yeah.

ANNE: Where is it?

MARCUS shows her a small scar under his right eye.

ANNE: Makes you look like a real man.

There's no need to thank me.

MARCUS: That isn't why I've come.

ANNE: You scared?

MARCUS: No.

Not Really.

You were pretty clear last time.

ANNE: The judge said I fucked you up well proper.

MARCUS: I don't think they were his exact words.

ANNE: Why didn't you fight back?

MARCUS: The judge praised me for it.

ANNE: You never even put up a fight. I thought what is he, some kind of pussy?

MARCUS: I knew you'd stop.

ANNE: Can't have been nice, to be fair, all them photos of you in the papers with me kicking your face in.

MARCUS: No.

ANNE: Done alright for yourself, haven't you? What qualifications do you need to be a prison officer? GCSEs? A-Levels?

MARCUS: A degree.

ANNE: I don't need a degree to kick your fucking head in.

MARCUS: If you try anything now, they'll be on you.

ANNE: I'm not gonna touch you. Six months I've been here and I've only just got a telly. This lot can't wait to take it off me.

MARCUS: What's your favourite programme?

ANNE: What?

MARCUS: On the telly, what do you watch?

ANNE: Who gives a fucking shit what my favourite fucking programme on the fucking telly is? Like I'd tell you that. Don't make small talk with me.

PRISON OFFICER approaches.

PRISON OFFICER: Everything alright?

MARCUS: Yes, thank you.

PRISON OFFICER: Start finishing off now please.

ANNE: You don't ever make small talk with me.

MARCUS: Okay. Okay.

ANNE: Where's your girlfriend?

MARCUS: You just said no small talk –

ANNE: How come she still wants to go out with you after what you done, that's what I don't get.

MARCUS: Do you wanna know something? I asked her that exact same question.

ANNE: Why didn't you fight back, Marcus?

PRISON OFFICER: End of visits now please. Sir. Mr Reeves, time's up.

MARCUS: I've got to go.

ANNE: Well this has been nice. To be fair, I've had better visits, but you take what you can get in here, do you know what I mean? Christ, I know how hard it is to get on a bus. And if the bus don't stop where you think it will – well that must have been a right fucking bastard. And all those doors to get in here. I noticed the doors too, you know. I was gonna go down Tesco's and get meself a scratch card the other day, but then I went hold on, someone's put all these doors in the way, and I can't get me scratch card cos I'm in a fucking prison aren't I? Well I'm glad I'm not the only one struggling with all the doors, Marcus. But you know, come back up some time, yeah? I'll have the kettle on.

MARCUS: I deserved it.

ANNE: And you can bring me a bleedin' scratch card n'all.

MARCUS: I didn't fight back because I deserved it.

ANNE: Yeah? Then why aren't you in here begging my forgiveness you piece of shit?

MARCUS: Would you forgive me?

ANNE: Everyone takes from me.

MARCUS: But I'm not the one who –

ANNE: I was in court you know.

MARCUS: Yes I've got the scar to prove it, haven't I? But I was found not guilty, Anne. The jury had all the evidence they could possibly need.

ANNE: It was on CCTV – I watched you do it.

MARCUS: Yes but I wasn't responsible.

ANNE: He told you he couldn't breathe. You knew.

MARCUS: Do you really think people would do that to a child on purpose? We were following a procedure, Anne. It was lawful. Tommy had kicked off –

ANNE: Don't say his name! You don't say his name!

MARCUS: He was out of control.

ANNE: I saw the whole thing plain as fucking day, but for some reason and I'm fucked if I know: not one fucking person is found guilty of murder or manslaughter or nothing.

MARCUS: What we did, Anne, was lawful and reasonable and –

ANNE: Oh this'll be good.

MARCUS: Appropriate.

ANNE: Appropriate?

MARCUS: Oh come on. Really? And what you did –

ANNE: What was appropriate?

MARCUS: The decisions we made.

ANNE: And I end up wearing the vest. Look at me in this fucking vest.

MARCUS: Why had he kicked off in the first place, Anne? Have you ever asked yourself that?

ANNE: It's like being in court again.

MARCUS: Two separate inquests, the CPS, some children's rights charity, they've all had a go and they got nowhere, that's all I'm saying. If you don't agree with the law, fine, but don't come blaming those who act on it.

ANNE: Telling me who *not* to blame comes so easy to you lot, don't it?

MARCUS: They made recommendations.

ANNE: Well I'll sleep better now, thank you.

MARCUS: I don't know what else you want me to say.

ANNE: He thought he could trust you.

MARCUS: Seriously. I don't know what else. Do you know what? This is a joke.

ANNE: He called for me, but you lied about that too.

MARCUS: He didn't call for you, Anne. I'm sorry but it didn't happen that way.

ANNE: He would've; I know he would've.

MARCUS: I know that's what you'd like to believe.

ANNE: Why did you come today?

MARCUS: You've been sending me V.O.s every fucking week.

ANNE: I know and you've never fucking come up, have you? So why today?

MARCUS: This isn't going to work. We tried but – I knew it was a bad idea – they said as much, but I wouldn't have it.

ANNE: Why did you come then?

MARCUS: I'm done.

ANNE: Please, Marcus. Why did you come?

MARCUS: I thought you wanted to apologise.

ANNE: Don't come here again.

MARCUS: Don't invite me again.

ANNE: Unless you got something different to say, don't you fucking dare come near me.

MARCUS: You sent me the V.O.s. What the hell do you think I'm gonna say when I get here?

ANNE: Why would I apologise to you?

Tommy was scared shitless every minute he was in there. And he knew. He knew you lot was after him.

MARCUS: When the other trainees found out what he did –

ANNE: I know what he did. I think about what he did every fucking day, Marcus. And then I think about what *you* did so don't try and tell me one is different from the other.

MARCUS: He was a complicated young man. And I know you must feel –

ANNE: If you say one more word I swear to God I will rip your face off.

MARCUS: Please, listen to me.

ANNE: Get your hands off me.

MARCUS: You say you want me to ask forgiveness from you and –

ANNE: Get out.

MARCUS: I need you to forgive me. I do need that.

ANNE: I said beg. Not ask.

MARCUS: But I was found not guilty, Anne, and what I'm saying is that if you could accept that, then we maybe could come together and talk. It's good that you asked me here, I should have come sooner, you're right, but we should talk about this and I don't know, some day, you know at some point, you might forgive me for my involvement but understand at the same time that I wasn't responsible.

ANNE: If you'd've done what you done outside in the street, you'd be in here wearing a vest like me.

MARCUS: I know that's what it must feel like. I was involved, I'm not saying I wasn't. I'm saying that I was found not guilty but I know I should be – well, I want to be – I mean, given what happened, it's quite right that I should come to you and –

ANNE: Get out.

MARCUS: I was so nervous coming here today. I've tried before. Fucking so many times, I get off the bus, but I can't get myself through the gates. I've been stood outside for two hours today, but I made myself come in. I was determined today. I was so nervous, but I was determined to do it, Anne. I have to explain what I said in court – I never meant to say it was his own fault, I'd never say that about a child, that isn't what I meant, but they learn the system these kids do, Anne, and it's hard on them, because sometimes they do just want a hug, as lame as that sounds – but they don't get hugs in places like prisons. It's not my job to go around giving hugs out, I kind of assume that's someone else's job, but they still crave that intimacy though – they crave being held, don't they? I'm sure they do. And I can see how you might think that came across as me blaming Tommy, I totally see that, but what I was trying to say was that sometimes kids engineer these situations that they know will result in restraint because what they really want is to be held and cuddled – contained, I guess, and that's what I meant when I said –

Sorry, I was so nervous coming here today.

MARCUS may be crying.

Forgive me. Please forgive me.

ANNE: When you are wearing this vest, and when I come through *that* door to visit *you*, then you can get on your knees and beg my forgiveness. You are a piece of shit.

MARCUS: I know.

ANNE: You murdered a child.

Live with it.

I do.

9.

TOMMY is in his cell. We hear voices from other prisoners directed at Tommy. 'String up, batty boy', and 'Batty boy won't see me coming'. 'Gonna wet you up, queer boy', 'Bang you out boss', 'I'll raze you up, swear down'. They bang their doors and the sound reverberates through TOMMY's cell. Eventually the abuse turns to wolf whistles and comments about 'sweet pussy' that follow someone walking up the corridor towards TOMMY's cell. The cell door opens. Enter SUE.

SUE: *(Shouts down corridor to trainees.)* I'm old enough to be your mother you filthy bastards.

Tommy, my darling.

TOMMY: Sorry about them lot, Sue.

SUE: Are you kidding? I'm going back for a lap of honour.

TOMMY: Sue!

SUE: Don't pretend to be all shocked with me, darling, you know me better than that.

So, I thought you were supposed to be segregated.

TOMMY: –

SUE: Tommy, is this going to be one of those visits when you don't speak, cos I've got thirty horny teenagers out there I could be tantalising.

TOMMY: I'll speak.

SUE: Good. Go on then.

TOMMY: What you wanna talk about?

SUE: The fighting.

TOMMY: Don't say it like that.

SUE: Is there another way you'd like me to say it?

TOMMY: Yeah.

SUE: Like what?

TOMMY: Like you care.

SUE: I'm sorry Tommy, do I not seem interested enough? It's Saturday night and I'm in your cell, does that seem like I don't care?

TOMMY: –

SUE: Why?

TOMMY: Dunno.

SUE: Prison's not like you thought it would be then.

TOMMY: I'm fine.

SUE: Boys who are fine don't start on prison officers, Tommy. Let me get this straight, ok? There's been some bullying, then you got restrained for some reason, I don't know, and next thing we know you're refusing to go into segregation.

TOMMY: Don't worry about it, Sue.

SUE: Why aren't you in segregation?

TOMMY: I said no.

SUE: You'll be safer there.

TOMMY: I'm under observation, innit.

SUE: Safer from them, not safer from you.

TOMMY: I ain't scared of them, Sue.

SUE: I spoke to Marcus.

TOMMY: Marcus is a dickhead, fam.

SUE: He's worried about you. Wants you to go into segregation tonight. That's why I'm here to try and talk you into it.

TOMMY: I ain't going.

SUE: Marcus said for me to tell you, that as much as he'd rather you went of your own free will, they can physically move you without your consent if they think it's in your best interests. You don't need to listen to this lot again.

TOMMY: I said I ain't scared of them.

SUE: And then there's this thing about the other fight yesterday. You want to tell me about that?

TOMMY: No.

SUE: Marcus says –

TOMMY: Marcus is chatting shit, fam. He's a fucking dickhead. I was gonna get twisted up by the govs and he stopped it. Fucking interfering prick is what he is.

SUE: I think it's good the govs didn't restrain you.

TOMMY: They should have twisted me up.

SUE: Marcus said he felt you were playing up on purpose –

TOMMY: So?

SUE: If you didn't like it the first time, why are you trying to get them to restrain you again?

TOMMY: Do you know what? Don't even bother, Sue.

SUE: Answer me.

TOMMY: Bare people was watching and they was gonna twist me up, right there in free association, with all of that lot watching. Then Marcus sticks his dickhead nose in and I don't even get put on basic.

SUE: He's looking out for you.

TOMMY: He's making it worse.

SUE: You start three fights in two days. What do you want?

TOMMY: I don't want to be in segregation innit.

SUE: You're not.

TOMMY: Marcus said he'd move me.

SUE: I'll talk to him.

TOMMY: If the govs wanna twist me up, then fucking let 'em. Man's not scared of some neek screws, blood. Man's a soldier. You see these beads, yeah? These are my own. Man's got his own beads, fam.

SUE: Marcus won't be able to stop it happening all the time.

TOMMY: I don't want him to stop it happening though do I?

SUE: It's not a good thing, Tommy.

TOMMY: The screws enjoy it.

SUE: That's not true.

TOMMY: They push you and push you till you snap, and you bang out cos they're on at you and they don't lay off.

SUE: I would believe that if it was true.

TOMMY: Broken bones and bruises is small tings, fam.

SUE: I'm not talking about broken bones. Just look at your mum, Tommy.

TOMMY: What about her?

SUE: Your mum –

TOMMY: Mum's normal.

SUE: You think? She got restrained a lot, Tommy. I don't want for you to get into a pattern where you feel – I guess I mean your mum used to try and make it happen on purpose and now you saying you want it as well, it feels like I've been here before and –

TOMMY: You get twisted up in here they leave you alone, that's the way it works.

SUE: I know that's what you think.

TOMMY: It's good. I like it.

SUE: You treat it like a badge of honour but it's not got you very far, has it?

TOMMY: Shut your mouth now, innit Sue.

SUE: Sorry Tommy, am I being too blunt? Is this too direct cos the last thing I'd like to do is upset you. Christ, Tommy you are a fucking idiot. You don't like it. You don't. These boys won't leave you alone because you've been restrained.

TOMMY: I like it. It feels – I dunno.

SUE: It feels what?

TOMMY: I'm learning to like the pain.

SUE: I can't have this conversation anymore. Do what you fucking like.

A natural lull in the conversation. SUE hesitates a moment, and then gets up and tries to give TOMMY a hug. TOMMY freezes, and does not reciprocate.

TOMMY: What the fuck are you doing?

SUE: I'm sorry. I just thought –

TOMMY: Don't fucking touch me.

SUE: Sure. Of course, I just thought –

TOMMY: What?

SUE: I just thought you might –

TOMMY: You lot ain't even allowed to touch me. I know my rights you know.

What you fucking go and do that for?

SUE: Because I thought it – never mind.

TOMMY: I'll go to segregation if it's what you want.

SUE: Good boy. Thank you.

Tommy, while I'm here there's one more thing I should say to you. When I come up in a couple of days, I'll bring your birthday present up, and your mum if she'll come. But you should also know that that will be my last time to see you. I'm leaving this job, so you'll have a new social worker. I know you will be delighted but I myself will miss you. This isn't the best time for you I see that but there never is a good time.

TOMMY: –

SUE: Is there anything you want to say?

TOMMY: –

SUE: I'll make sure your new social worker knows all about you.

TOMMY: I don't want a new social worker.

SUE: I can't do anything about that, I'm afraid.

TOMMY: Where are you going?

SUE: I don't like to discuss my personal life.

TOMMY: I discuss mine with you.

SUE: You do. And it's quite a life, it really is.

My daughter has just had a baby, and she's not coping very well. So I'm going up there to help out.

That was too much information, I'm really sorry.

TOMMY: I ain't talking to you no more.

SUE: Okay.

TOMMY: I mean it. You can go fuck yourself.

SUE: Just steady on, would you?

TOMMY: Why are you leaving me?

SUE: In any case, I think it might be better for you to have a different social worker.

TOMMY: You've been my social worker for time though, innit Sue?

SUE: And look what good it's done you.

TOMMY: Don't be dumb.

SUE: Fucking hell, Tommy. Fucking hell. Look at you.

TOMMY: What's wrong with me?

SUE: Can I ask you a question, Tommy?

TOMMY: You always ask me questions.

SUE: I'd like to know what you think.

TOMMY: Of what?

SUE: Of everything. I'd like to know why you don't hate me for starters.

TOMMY: I do.

SUE: Good. Thank you. I think you should.

TOMMY: I ain't talking to you no more.

SUE: Well maybe you'll talk to your new social worker.

TOMMY: I don't want a new social worker.

SUE: I'm sorry, Tommy. There's never a good time to leave.

TOMMY: Don't talk to me I said I ain't talking to you no more.

SUE: I'll be up in a couple of days. We'll have a proper goodbye then.

TOMMY: –

SUE: I'm one week away from leaving. I don't want any more professional highlights from you.

TOMMY: Am I still your number one?

SUE: The wheelie bin?

TOMMY: Innit.

SUE: You are right to hate me. I think you should.

10.

An office in the prison. MARCUS, TOMMY and SUE. There are CCTV cameras and a telephone.

MARCUS: Okay. So, Tommy, I know it's not till next week, but I thought that as Sue's up today, I figure we could say happy birthday now.

SUE: And give you your present.

TOMMY: –

SUE: You normally get £80, don't you? But as you can't spend all that in here, we got you these instead.

SUE produces a Nike trainer box.

MARCUS: If they're not the right ones, let us know – it's no problem to –

SUE: – Or if they don't fit

TOMMY: Mum was supposed to bring in my ones from home.

MARCUS: I know. Why don't you save them ones for when you're back with mum? These ones'll do for in here.

SUE: Do you like them?

TOMMY: –

MARCUS: Tommy, do you like them?

TOMMY: They ain't like my old ones.

SUE: That's okay. You can have two different styles.

TOMMY puts them on.

TOMMY: Thanks, yeah.

MARCUS: No worries, mate. You deserve a treat. And they look good, right Sue? Very cool.

SUE: Don't get them nicked.

MARCUS: Yeah, and if you sell them –

TOMMY: I ain't gonna sell them.

MARCUS: You heard it here first, Sue. Shall we embarrass him and sing, Sue?

TOMMY: Nah that's gay, man.

MARCUS: I've been practising.

TOMMY: Swear you ain't gonna sing.

SUE: Tommy, what's your problem? We wanna sing.

MARCUS: Maybe just quietly?

MARCUS and SUE begin a very hushed rendition of Happy Birthday. *TOMMY squirms and gets more and more uncomfortable.*

TOMMY: Shut up! What's wrong with you? Dickheads.

MARCUS: Woah woah woah, sit down mate, we've stopped now.

SUE: Er, Tommy, don't be shouting at us please.

TOMMY: What you singing for?

SUE: We've stopped.

TOMMY: Yeah but you *were* singing.

MARCUS: Were we that bad?

The phone rings.

TOMMY: Don't take the piss out of me.

SUE: He's not, Tom –

TOMMY: And don't sing. It's jarring man.

SUE: We're done with the singing. Okay?

TOMMY: Fucking singing. Batty.

An awkward gap in conversation with the phone still in background.

MARCUS: Sue, is there anything else you need to discuss with Tommy?

SUE: Nope, I'm gonna call mum and get a date to bring her up.

MARCUS: Why don't you leave me with this bundle of joy then, Sue?

SUE: Good. Right then. I guess that's me done here. Tommy, you got anything else you want to discuss?

TOMMY: –

MARCUS: Tommy?

TOMMY: No.

SUE: Okay then. So, Tommy, this is goodbye, isn't it? It's been a pleasure, it really has.

TOMMY: Bring my mum next time.

SUE: Tommy, I won't be coming again. Your new social worker will bring her. This is where we say goodbye.

TOMMY: Don't bother coming if you ain't got her with you.

SUE: Tommy my darling, it would be good if we could say goodbye nicely.

TOMMY: Fuck off then.

MARCUS: Right. Now you're being rude.

SUE: It's alright, Marcus. Tommy, I wish you all the best.

MARCUS: Just go to that door, they'll sort you out.

SUE: Bye Tommy.

TOMMY: –

SUE: You don't make it easy for us, do you Tommy? Goodbye darling.

SUE goes to hug TOMMY, but hesitates and decides against it. She walks to the door and is let out by GUARDS. TOMMY makes a gun shape with his hand and 'shoots' Sue.

MARCUS: Right you. Back to your cell.

TOMMY: It's free association.

MARCUS: Not for you, it isn't. And where are your manners?

Suddenly TOMMY angrily rips the trainers off his feet and throws them into their box with such force they end up strewn. MARCUS deliberately stands back, calm and unaffected by this performance. TOMMY runs back and picks up the shoes, wrapping them neatly in the paper and putting them gently into the box.

TOMMY: Has the letter come?

MARCUS: What letter?

TOMMY: From me mum.

MARCUS: You've not had any post today mate.

TOMMY: She said she was gonna write.

MARCUS: Who, your mum? Maybe it'll get here tomorrow. Hang on, while I check this message will you.

MARCUS picks up the phone, enters the code and listens to the answerphone message.

TOMMY: If she didn't come she said she'd write, and send me fucking trainers.

TOMMY flings them to the floor.

MARCUS: Pick them up will you.

TOMMY: Is it her?

MARCUS: *(Gesturing to the trainers.)* Er, excuse me.

TOMMY: Is that my mum?

MARCUS: It is, yeah but –

TOMMY: Let me listen, Marcus, man. She shoulda come though innit, but she called so that's better than nothing. She's probably got no cash.

MARCUS: She's not saying much to be honest.

TOMMY: Doesn't matter, man. Let me just listen.

MARCUS: Leave it for now, Tommy, she's not saying much.

TOMMY: Innit she ran out of cash, Marcus?

MARCUS: Pick your trainers up mate, then we'll get you back.

TOMMY: Can I listen to the message from my mum, please?

MARCUS: It's not –

TOMMY: Hurry up, it'll be finished soon.

MARCUS hesitates. TOMMY is crowding him. A moment. A choice. MARCUS passes the phone to TOMMY. TOMMY listens.

Eventually, he puts the phone down.

MARCUS: Mate, she sounded–

TOMMY: Don't talk to me. Don't fucking talk to me.

MARCUS: Mate, look just pick your trainers up, we'll get you back, and then I'll come and give her a call. See what's what.

TOMMY: I don't want your batty trainers, you're a dickhead.

MARCUS: I didn't ask if you wanted them, I said pick them up.

TOMMY: No.

MARCUS: Tommy –

TOMMY: *She* shoulda brung them.

MARCUS: Maybe she didn't have the money this month. Pick 'em up and I'll take you back to your cell.

TOMMY: I ain't pickin' them up.

MARCUS: Tommy, pick up your trainers, please.

TOMMY: You pick 'em up.

MARCUS: Tommy, you threw them there, you pick them up.

TOMMY: You do it, you fuckin' pick them up you cunt. Oh my days, you're a prick.

MARCUS: That's enough out of you, pick up the trainers now or they're going in the bin.

TOMMY: Do you see me pickin' them up? Do you see me pickin' up your batty trainers? Do you see me pickin' up your trainers, do you see me picking them up?

MARCUS: I don't care if you want them or not, they've got to be moved from there. I know you're upset, Tommy, but...

TOMMY: Do you see me pickin' up the trainers?

Repeats as MARCUS says:

MARCUS: Fine, it's the bin then.

TOMMY: Do I look like I want your neek trainers? *(Repeats this.)*

MARCUS: Last chance. If they go in the bin you won't see them again.

TOMMY: Do you think I want that shit? Do you think I want it?

MARCUS picks up the trainers, puts them in the box and dumps them in the bin. TOMMY runs to the bin to try and get them. MARCUS stands in front of the bin and blocks him.

MARCUS: Get back would you?

TOMMY starts pummelling him. MARCUS is acting defensively, blocking the blows and trying to keep him at arm's reach as TOMMY tries to get to the trainers.

TOMMY: Gimme them... Gimme my trainers...they're mine, give 'em back.

MARCUS: They *were* yours.

TOMMY: I'm gonna fuck you up. I swear down I'm gonna fuck you up.

MARCUS: Tommy, mate, you're upset. Your mum was –

TOMMY: Don't say my fucking mum, you don't know my fucking mum.

ALEX and LOU enter and grab TOMMY by each arm. With considerable force, they drag him across the room and pin him against the wall. MARCUS gets the trainers out the bin, takes them to TOMMY, then walks back and slams them back into the bin.

TOMMY screams and begins to struggle. Tears run down his face. TOMMY struggles continuously throughout.

TOMMY: They're mine!

ALEX: That's enough out of you.

LOU: Don't be starting on us.

This sends TOMMY over. His struggles are more violent. He lashes out, screams a tirade of abuse. After a few moments he escapes their grip and runs to the bin. He is tripped up and as he tries to get the trainers he is pulled back across the floor by his feet. He screams from the gut and his tirade of ad lib abuse continues.

Stop this!

MARCUS: Guys, let's see if we can calm him down, can we? He's vulner –

ALEX: Not again, Marcus.

TOMMY is lashing out violently. Ad lib.

LOU: He's out of control. I'll get his thumbs.

MARCUS: We don't need that. Not yet.

They can barely contain TOMMY.

Okay. He's not safe.

MARCUS and the TWO GUARDS manoeuvre TOMMY into a position where they can reach his thumbs. ALEX gets one of TOMMY's thumbs in each of his hands and twists them. TOMMY screams from the pain and it enrages him further. His ad lib tirade continues.

ALEX: We are the boss. We have control. When they send you here you have no control.

MARCUS: Okay, Tommy. Happy now? Can we let you go so we can get you back to your cell?

TOMMY spits in MARCUS' face.

LOU: Woah, woah, no. You're making a twat of yourself you little shit.

MARCUS: It's okay guys, I'm not bothered.

ALEX: You don't do that to us.

MARCUS: Just keep him there for a bit, see if he tires himself out.

ALEX: Can we get him sat down?

MARCUS: Grab the seat and he can wear himself out. Tommy, I'll know you're ready for us to start letting go when you take two deep breaths. That will show me you are ready to take control of yourself in a safe way.

TOMMY's ad lib tirade continues.

LOU: On three. One. Two. Three. Marcus, you –

A surge of resistance from TOMMY.

MARCUS: What?

LOU: Just get him sat down.

MARCUS and the TWO GUARDS push TOMMY down towards a chair. TOMMY resists in every way possible, but they eventually get him sat on a chair. They hold his arms and push him forward so he is almost doubled over. MARCUS is at TOMMY's head. TOMMY is screaming, GUARDS ad lib things like 'If you keep still we can let you go', 'That's enough, settle down would you?' TOMMY becomes more and more ad lib abusive all the while they hold him in the position. After some considerable time, his ad lib abuse turns into…

TOMMY: I can't breathe, please, I can't breathe – please let go of me. I mean it, I swear down, I can't breathe. I'm not lying I'm not lying, I swear I ain't lying.

ALEX: I'd really like for us to let go of Tommy, Marcus, but we can't do that until he's shown us he's back in control of himself.

MARCUS: Tommy, when you are in control of yourself, we'd like to let go of you.

ALEX: Let him wear himself out. Do you remember what you're in here for?

TOMMY: I'm gonna be sick, please, I'm gonna be sick, I can't breathe, Marcus, get off me, Marcus.

TOMMY vomits.

ALEX: Do you remember what you done? Do you?

LOU: What's his head like, Marcus?

MARCUS: Yep.

TOMMY: I'm gonna poo, please stop, I need to shit, I'm gonna shit myself.

ALEX: No he's not.

TOMMY screams louder and shits himself. His face is red, his eyes are bulging.

What's wrong with this one?

MARCUS: Give him some space guys, his breathing is –

LOU: He's not calm yet. His breathing's what?

MARCUS: He looks –

LOU: You're not supposed to stop midway if you –

MARCUS: Now.

TOMMY: Marcus... Please, Marcus, you're hurting me, I can't breathe. Get them off me, I can't breathe. Please stop. Marcus. I'm sorry, just stop, fuck, just fucking stop please. Marcus. Marcus, I can't breathe. Mum. Marcus. I can't breathe.

TOMMY's breath becomes shorter and his struggles become infrequent and less powerful, his face is ashen and he begins to have a seizure. At this point GUARDS let go of TOMMY. TOMMY slumps to the floor. TOMMY remains in seizure on the floor, choking. And then stops breathing entirely.

LOU: Fuck. Is he okay?

MARCUS: I don't know. Turn him over.

ALEX: Radio healthcare.

MARCUS checks for vital signs.

LOU: Jesus. Is he okay?

ALEX: Is he breathing?

MARCUS: I think so, I don't know.

ALEX: Well fucking check.

MARCUS: What do you think I'm doing? He's not moving. Fuck. I can't feel anything. Where's the fucking nurse?

ALEX: Tommy? You got a pulse, Marcus.

MARCUS: I don't know.

LOU: I'm gonna do CPR. Move, would you.

ALEX and LOU begin CPR. MARCUS steps back, out of the scene, almost as if he's dreaming it, and stares up into the CCTV camera.

11.

A children's playground on a bright autumn day. Children can be heard enjoying the surroundings. MARCUS sits on a bench. Next to him is an empty pushchair.

Enter ANNE. She keeps her distance until MARCUS notices her.

MARCUS: Anne.

ANNE: Alright.

MARCUS: What are you?

God, I'm really, er, – Hi.

Hello.

Pause.

ANNE: Nice park.

MARCUS: Yes, it is, isn't it?

ANNE: I'd never come before I got out.

MARCUS: It's funny – the things on your doorstep – often you don't –

ANNE: No.

MARCUS: How long have you–?

ANNE: A while.

MARCUS: And you're back in your old flat?

ANNE: Live round here now.

MARCUS: Oh. I'm surprised we haven't–

ANNE: Really?

MARCUS: Better that way, maybe, do you not think?

ANNE: Why?

MARCUS: Well – you know. Do you really want to keep running into me? I mean – if –

ANNE: If you was me.

MARCUS: Exactly. If I were you I wouldn't want to keep running into me.

ANNE: We've managed so far.

MARCUS: Maybe I should –

ANNE: Can I sit with you, Marcus?

MARCUS: I'm not sure that's a good idea. Are we even allowed?

ANNE: You got nothing to say now. Is that it?

MARCUS: I'm not sure this is a good idea, that's all.

ANNE: What are you scared of?

MARCUS: I'm not scared of you, if that's what you're asking.

It was good to see you, Anne.

ANNE: Marcus, please. I'm not like that anymore. Sit with me a bit, yeah?

MARCUS: Why?

ANNE: Small talk.

MARCUS: You always said no small talk.

ANNE: I'm better at it now. It might do us good, you never know.

MARCUS: I don't think it will.

ANNE: Two minutes. About the weather and shit.

MARCUS: Two minutes. Then I really need to go.

ANNE: Two minutes of small talk. That's all I want.

MARCUS: Okay.

ANNE: Okay.

Go on then.

MARCUS: Why do I have to start?

ANNE: It's gentlemanly.

MARCUS: Fine – whatever. How are you keeping, Anne?

ANNE: Fine, thank you.

You?

MARCUS: I'm okay. Thank you.

ANNE: See? It ain't so hard. How's what's-her-name?

MARCUS: You said small talk.

ANNE: That is small talk.

MARCUS: If I'm being honest with you, I'm not sure I'm totally comfortable answering that.

ANNE: Don't be such a twat. Answer the question.

MARCUS: It's lovely out today. They said rain, but we've been okay so far.

ANNE: She dumped you then. So go on. Why'd she dump you?

MARCUS: Anne. I'm not getting into this–

ANNE: Was is after what you done?

MARCUS: It's none of your business.

ANNE: Did she wake up one morning and realise she couldn't even look at you?

MARCUS: I left her.

ANNE: I don't believe you.

MARCUS: I woke up the morning of my trial, I looked at her and she disgusted me so I left her. There's your small talk.

ANNE: Why?

Marcus, why?

MARCUS: I brought the brolly just in case. You can never tell these days. And what about you, Anne?

ANNE: Not much to say.

MARCUS: Things have changed. I don't know if that's of any help to you.

ANNE: –

MARCUS: Why wouldn't you see me again? After that first time, I came every week.

ANNE: I know.

MARCUS: I thought we were getting somewhere.

ANNE: Getting where, Marcus? Where was we getting?

MARCUS: Why wouldn't you come down?

This hasn't left me, Anne.

ANNE: Because I sussed out why you kept wanting to see me.

MARCUS: Was that so bad?

ANNE: You look like you've moved on okay if you ask me. On to the next one and all that.

MARCUS: No.

ANNE: No?

MARCUS: No, I haven't moved on. What do you want me say? It's been two years. I'm not sat in the prison begging you to come out your cell and talk to me anymore, no, you're right, but do you think that means I'm over it?

ANNE: You never begged me.

MARCUS: You're obsessed. I bet you'd loved it if I did. It would give you such a power trip having the system suck up to you.

ANNE: Well the system's got to take care of someone.

MARCUS: I did not fucking do it, Anne, okay? It was not my fault. And you can't separate yourself from the fact that you raised a boy who was so fucked up that he –

ANNE: I know what he did. It's flung in my face often enough.

MARCUS: I wasn't talking about that, Anne. I liked Tommy. What they've done never matters to me –

ANNE: I don't believe that.

MARCUS: – But what I mean is you have to really screw up a kid for him to get to that point. That's the boy you raised.

ANNE: I was never allowed to raise that boy.

MARCUS: Rubbish. That's all people ever wanted you to do. Sue gave you more chances than anyone to keep him.

ANNE: They forced him on me. They took him off me then forced him back on me.

MARCUS: Oh here we go. I've heard this one before. Poor you. It's everyone's fault except yours. Well that's fucking original. And you've got an opinion on everything, haven't you? I'd like to see you come and work with me for a day. You wouldn't last five minutes. Cos it's hard Anne, it's hard looking after fucked-up children that fucked-up people like you have fucked up so much that they end up in a fucked-up system like this. You didn't want anything to do with your kid –

ANNE: So why did –

MARCUS: Nothing. You abused him, you never once visited –

ANNE: Yeah so why did they keep sending him back to me?

MARCUS: Because you're his fucking mother. And then you abandon the boy, you fucking palm him off onto us and then have the fucking audacity to criticise the job we're doing. Two years ago I needed you to forgive me, Anne, it would have meant the world, but now all I want is for people like you – do you know what? Forget it.

ANNE: People like me?

MARCUS: I said forget about it.

ANNE: People like me? You want people like me to what?

MARCUS: You can't win this. I don't know if maybe you think I won and you lost, but believe me I have not won. I will never forgive myself for this, so how dare you? How fucking dare you?

ANNE: They should of just left him, Marcus. You and all.

MARCUS: We were trying to –

ANNE: I know what you was all trying to do. I've read my files. There's seventy-three files about me and I have read every single one so I know what you lot thought you was trying to do. Am I supposed to be grateful? We didn't stand a chance. We was watched – everyday, we was watched. Every little tiny thing and they couldn't wait for me to fuck up. And of course I fucked up, and they loved it when I did cos it just gave them more power. One day I could have him, and the next day I couldn't, and if I did this he'd be allowed back, but if I didn't he wasn't. Do you know what that is Marcus? It's torture. It is absolute torture and I've had a life full of it. You lot think I'm a dog. You think I'm a fucking dog.

MARCUS: This is exactly what I'm talking about. You can't take any fucking responsibility, can you? We have to live with it, Anne. We *all* have to live with it.

ANNE: I was the best mum I could be.

MARCUS: Where you going next, Anne? Gonna turn up at Sue's front door and give her a talking to as well? Is this gonna be an annual fixture, because I know what day it is, Anne, I don't need you jumping out the fucking bushes to remind me what day it is. Jesus.

I can't listen to this anymore. I've got my son to look after.

ANNE: He looks like you, you know.

MARCUS: Whatever, Anne.

ANNE: And he started walking early.

MARCUS: For his age he did, I know. So what? What the fuck are you on about, Anne?

ANNE: Looks just like you he does. It's hard to keep up with them when you only see them at weekends. You miss out on so much.

Is she picking him up the usual time tonight?

Pause.

MARCUS: *(Without fear.)* I can't give you what you need, Anne. Not anymore.

We're going now.

Michael!

Michael!

Come get your coat on, buddy.

Michael!

ANNE: Tommy!

MARCUS: *(As he exits.)* Michael!

ANNE: Tommy.

MARCUS: Look at the mess on you.

ANNE: Tommy! Get away from that slide, Tommy. It ain't your turn. Get here, now. Tommy. Tommy!

TOMMY appears. There is no time and there is no place.

ANNE: Come here, son.

ANNE and TOMMY embrace.

TOMMY: Will you bring my trainers?

ANNE: Yeah.

TOMMY: I'll write though.

ANNE: It's alright, Tommy.

TOMMY: Me Nike ones, yeah?

ANNE: They'll get robbed.

TOMMY: No they won't, come visit me, mum, yeah?

ANNE: *(Tightens her embrace.)* Come 'ere.

TOMMY: I can't breathe, Mum!

ANNE: Don't lie.

TOMMY: Me Nike ones, mum, yeah?

ANNE: Yeah, your Nike ones, I know.

TOMMY: When will you come up?

ANNE: Soon.

TOMMY: I'll write, mum.

ANNE: Me too.

TOMMY: You'll come up though?

ANNE: Yeah, I'll be up.

TOMMY: When though?

ANNE: Soon. Dunno.

TOMMY: With me trainers?

ANNE squeezes him tighter still.

TOMMY: Mum? Me trainers, mum.

ANNE: I know, Tommy.

TOMMY: Mum. I can't breathe.